B is for Beaver

An Oregon Alphabet

Written by Marie and Roland Smith
Illustrated by Michael Roydon

Sleeping Bear Press
310 North Main Street, Suite 300
Chelsea, MI 48118
www.sleepingbearpress.com

Sleeping Bear Press is an imprint of The Gale Group, Inc.,
a business of The Thomson Corporation.

Printed and bound in China.

10 9 8 7 6 5 4 3 2

Library of Congress Cataloging-in-Publication Data
Smith, Marie, 1951-
B is for beaver : an Oregon alphabet / written by Marie and Roland Smith ;
illustrated by Michael Roydon.
p. cm.
Summary: Each letter of the alphabet is illustrated by objects
that are associated with the State of Oregon and accompanied
by background information.
ISBN 1-58536-071-6
1. Oregon—Juvenile literature. 2. English language—Alphabet
Juvenile literature. [1. Oregon. 2. Alphabet.] I. Smith, Roland, 1951- .
II. Roydon, Michael, 1952- , ill. III. Title.
F876.3.S65 2002
979.5[E]—dc21   2002012753

For Willingham Gillis Culpepper,
the newest member of our family alphabet.

MARIE & ROLAND

✺

To my sis Mish.
You're with me.

MIKE

Aa

Astoria is the oldest American settlement west of the Rockies. Originally, Astoria was a fur trading fort named after John Jacob Astor who paid to have the fort built in 1811. Fort Astoria depended on Native Americans and trappers to supply it with furs. The fort helped establish the United State's claim to the Oregon territory when the United States and Great Britain disagreed over ownership. In 1846 a compromise called The Oregon Treaty gave America the land south of the 49th parallel and Britain the land north of the parallel. This line is the border between the United States and Canada.

The Corps of Discovery led by Captain Meriwether Lewis and Captain William Clark spent the winter of 1805-06 southeast of Astoria. They named their stockade Fort Clatsop after a Native American tribe in the area.

The Astoria bridge, over four miles long, is the world's longest continuous truss bridge. It connects Oregon and Washington across the Columbia River.

A is for Astoria,
a fort built long ago.
Trappers and Native Americans
helped to make it grow.

B is for the "Beaver State,"
Oregon's other name.
Trapped to near extinction,
the beaver still remains.

The beaver is North America's largest rodent and was adopted as our state animal in 1969. Baby beaver are called kits and grow up to 4 feet in length and weigh up to 65 pounds. Adapted to live in water, beavers have a paddle-shaped tail, webbed hind feet, valves that close their ears and nose, and an oil gland that waterproofs their fur. Nicknamed "nature's engineer," beavers build dams that help with water flow and control soil from washing away. Their dome-shaped homes built on the water are called lodges and are made out of branches, sticks, and mud. Inside the lodge is a room that keeps them warm and dry. Beavers are primarily nocturnal, which means they are most active at night.

Years ago hats made out of beaver fur were very fashionable. Oregon became the main source for these furs. Luckily, fashion changed and a law in the early 1900s was enacted to save the beaver from extinction.

On July 4, 1909, the people of Pendleton held a celebration with bronco riding, races, greased pig catching, and fireworks. They had such a good time they decided to do it every year and the Pendleton Roundup was born with the slogan *Let'er Buck!* The annual get-together was eventually moved to the middle of September when local farmers and ranchers had more time to participate. The Pendleton Roundup is now one of the top rodeos in the world.

C is also for Chinook salmon, our state fish. Salmon are an important part of Oregon's history and economy. The first salmon cannery on the Columbia River was built in 1866. Chinook salmon are the largest species of salmon in Oregon. Mature fish range from two pounds to more than 70 pounds. Salmon hatch in freshwater then migrate to the ocean where they spend their adult lives. They return to where they were spawned to lay their eggs.

C is for Cowboys
and also for Clowns.
The Pendleton Roundup
brings them both to town.

D is for Douglas fir
Oregon's state tree.
Tall up to the sky it grows.
Tilt far back to see.

The Douglas fir was named after botanist David Douglas who identified the tree in 1825. He was sent by the Royal Horticultural Society to find trees that would be useful for landscaping in England. The Douglas fir is found throughout Oregon and is one of the biggest trees in the world. Nearly half of our state is covered with trees and many of them are Douglas fir.

The Douglas fir grows very straight and is said to be harder than concrete. It's used to make telephone poles and railroad ties. Builders use it to frame houses, churches, and schools. The tree is also found in homes during the holidays. Oregon produces more Christmas trees than any other state and families find the Douglas fir a favorite to decorate.

The Rocky Mountain Douglas Fir National Champion is located in Deschutes National Forest near the Jefferson Lake Trail. This champion tree is 24 feet around and 114 feet tall.

Dd

E e

E is for Egg,
but not the kind you eat.
Oregon's rock is the Thunder Egg,
made by volcanic heat.

The thunder egg was adopted as our state rock in 1965. They are plain on the outside but inside have a variety of beautiful designs and vibrant colors. They are 20-40 million years old.

According to Native American legend, the rocks come from the Thunder Spirits who lived on the peaks of Mount Hood and Mount Jefferson. During thunder and lightning storms they fought and threw the massive eggs of the mythical thunderbird at each other. Millions of thunder eggs are scattered at the base of these mountains.

Our most famous rock is not a thunder egg but a meteorite. The Willamette Meteorite was discovered by farmer and miner Ellis Hughes in 1902. Scientists believe it originated in the asteroid belt between Mars and Jupiter before hitting the small community of Willamette 10 thousand years ago. The size of a small car, it weighs 30 thousand pounds and is the largest meteorite ever found in the United States.

Ff

The John Day Fossil Beds National Monument was established in 1975. This 14,000-acre park is divided into three separate units: Sheep Rock, Clarno, and the Painted Hills. Over 40 million years of Oregon history can be seen in these rock formations. They are the richest fossil beds in North America. This area was once a semitropical forest and home to over a hundred different animal species including saber-toothed tigers, camels, sloths, and rhinoceros. The Clarno unit has fossils of over 300 plant species. The colorful streaks in the Painted Hills unit were created by volcanic ash erosion. The Sheep Rock unit has a museum featuring exhibits of fossils.

Thomas Condon was a pioneer, teacher, author, clergyman, and geologist who came to Oregon as a missionary in 1853. He was the first scientist to study the fossils in the John Day region and became Oregon's first state geologist.

F is for Fossils.
Find them near John Day.
Camels, sloths, or saber-tooth,
their prints are on display.

Gg

The Columbia River Gorge is 80 miles long and up to 4,000 feet deep. The river is an important means of transportation through the Cascade Mountains. One of the most visited areas along the gorge is Multnomah Falls. Fed by underground springs from Larch Mountain it cascades 620 feet down to rocky pools, making it the second highest year-round waterfall in the United States. On November 17, 1986, President Ronald Reagan signed into law an act creating the Columbia River Gorge National Scenic Area. It is our nation's only National Scenic Area. The Historic Columbia River Highway was the first modern highway in Oregon and the first scenic highway in the United States.

G is also for our state flower, the Oregon Grape, which grows throughout the state.

G is for the Gorge
where the Columbia River runs.
See rocky cliffs, waterfalls,
and windsurfers having fun.

The Hells Canyon Wilderness area runs along the Oregon and Idaho border. Here the canyon is nearly 8,000 feet deep which makes it the deepest canyon in North America and the deepest river gorge in the world. Plans were made to build a dam across the Snake River in the area of Hells Canyon but no one could decide who should do it. A man named Floyd Harvey didn't want a dam at all. He started contacting people to stop the dam. The question was eventually brought before the Supreme Court. The court ruled that the Federal Power Commission should give greater consideration to not building the dam at all! It was a wonderful surprise which gave Floyd Harvey more time to persuade people that it should be left alone.

On December 31, 1975, a 71-mile stretch of the Snake River through Hells Canyon became a National Recreation Area preserving this beautiful place.

H h

H is for Hells Canyon.
Did you know?
It's one of the deepest in the world.
Watch out below!

I i

Crater Lake was created when Mount Mazuma erupted over 6,000 years ago. At 1,932 feet deep, it's the deepest lake in the United States. Wizard and Phantom Ship are two islands that appear to float on top of the lake. The blue waters come only from snow and rain.

In the mid 1800s a Kansas schoolboy named William Gladstone Steel read about Crater Lake in a newspaper used to wrap his lunch. William's dream was to see the lake for himself. When he was 18 years old his family moved to Portland and 13 years later his dream came true. In August 1885, William stood on the rim of Crater Lake. He was so moved by the beauty of the lake he began campaigning and gathering signatures to protect the area. In 1902 President Theodore Roosevelt signed a bill making Crater Lake Oregon's only national park. Without William Gladstone Steel's dream and hard work it might not have happened.

I is for Island.
Crater Lake has two—
        Wizard and Phantom Ship
on top a lake so blue.

The Nez Perce tribe lived in the Wallowa Valley in northeast Oregon. Early settlers wanted to farm this fertile valley, so the federal government tried to purchase the land from the tribe. The Nez Perce refused and the government ordered them onto a reservation. They fled to the safety of Canada. Just before reaching the border, soldiers captured most of them. In the end they were forced onto a reservation.

Upon surrendering, Chief Joseph told the soldiers, "It is cold and we have no blankets. The little children are freezing to death... Hear me, my chiefs! I am tired. My heart is sick and sad. From where the sun now stands I will fight no more forever." Chief Joseph never again lived in the Wallowa Valley.

There is now a town in the Wallowa Valley named after Chief Joseph. Joseph is an artist community and a recreational area. Hot air balloonists have found this valley one of the nicest views ever.

Jj

J is for Joseph,
    a Nez Perce tribal chief.
They took his land forever,
    causing his people grief.

K k

A horse of a different color
is what some people say
about the Kiger mustang
which starts with the letter **K**.

Kiger mustangs were found in the high desert area near the Steens Mountains. For years they were forgotten in this rough and remote part of Oregon. The horses are believed to be the most pure descendants of the ancient Spanish breeds first brought to North America by the conquistadors centuries ago. Named after Kiger Gorge, they are now sought after for their beautiful and unusual coloring. They sell for thousands of dollars.

K is also for the Klamath Basin. Upper Klamath Lake, located in this basin, is our largest lake and one of the best bird-watching areas in the state. Canada geese, pintails, mallards, American White pelican, double-crested cormorant, heron, and other birds use this lake during their annual migrations. The basin also has the largest number of wintering bald eagles in the lower 48 states.

L is for Lion
with a different kind of roar.
These live and play in caves
along our rocky shore.

The Sea Lion Caves located on Oregon's coast are the largest in the United States. Over 25 million years old, the main cave is as long as a football field and about as tall as a 12-story building. Hundreds of Steller sea lions live in the safety of this natural sanctuary.

Steller sea lions are marine mammals. They gather inside the caves during fall and winter. During spring and summer they have babies on the rocky ledges outside. The babies (called pups) weigh 40 to 50 pounds and are about four feet long. They grow rapidly and can reach six feet in one year. Females (called cows) average nine feet in length and weigh up to seven hundred pounds. The males (called bulls) average twelve feet in length and can weigh up to one ton. They eat mainly fish, squid, and octopus.

In December of 1972 the federal government created a law prohibiting the killing, harassment, and capture of any marine mammal.

M is for Marionberries,
an original Oregon sweet.
    Eat them plain or make a pie,
a perfect summer treat.

Marionberries are Oregon's number one caneberry crop and are in demand all over the world. George Waldo, a berry breeder with the Agricultural Research Service in Oregon, developed them. The berry is a cross between two other blackberries, the Chehalem and the Olallie. Marionberries have small seeds and an excellent flavor. They were named after Marion County where they were first tested in 1956. Oregon is the leading producer of caneberries in the United States.

Our state beverage is milk. Drink a tall glass of cold milk with a piece of pie!

M is also for McLoughlin. Dr. John McLoughlin is known as the "Father of Oregon." He was given this title because he helped so many pioneers after their hard journey across the Oregon Trail. The Native Americans called him the "White Headed Eagle" because of his white flowing hair. His house is located in Oregon City and is now a museum and national historic site.

M
m

N n

Bill Bowerman was born in Fossil and graduated from the University of Oregon where he was a coach for 24 years. He is known as the man who brought jogging to America. A kitchen waffle iron gave him an idea—he would make shoes with waffle soles to run faster. Phil Knight was a member of Coach Bowerman's team and later became his business partner. Together they started a company called Nike. Nike was named for the Greek goddess of victory.

Oregon may have the newest in athletic shoes, but it also has the oldest shoes. A pair of 10,000-year-old sagebrush sandals were discovered in Oregon. These sandals are the oldest shoes ever found in North America.

Our state nut is the hazelnut but many Oregonians prefer to call it a filbert. Oregon supplies 99% of the world's hazelnuts. That's a lot of nuts!

N is for Nike,
one coach's dream
about a better shoe
to help his team.

BEAVERTON

EUGENE

FORT ROCK

The Oregon Trail was the largest voluntary human migration in history, bringing over 300,000 pioneers to the western frontier during the 1800s. It was called "Oregon Fever." Starting in Missouri, the journey was over 2,000 miles long. Some pioneers had wagons but most walked the entire way. Two women important to Oregon's history came over this busy trail.

Abigail Scott Duniway traveled to Oregon when she was seventeen. Her mother and youngest brother died along the way. She became a schoolteacher, married, and had several children. She started a newspaper called the *New Northwest*, becoming an active spokesperson for women's right to vote. In 1912, at age 78, she became the first woman to vote in Oregon.

Tabitha Moffatt Brown, a widow, came to Oregon when she was 66 years old. She started a home and school for orphans that eventually became Pacific University, now located in Forest Grove. She was called the "Mother of Oregon" for her charitable and compassionate work.

O is for the Oregon Trail
bringing wagonloads of pioneers
traveling from Missouri
with plans for new frontiers.